Watch the TED talk that inspired this book, where
I talk about BEing yourself, active listening, defining
"your" success, and growing the "right" audience.
Expect a handful of AHAs when
watching and listening to this TED Talk:
http://aha.pub/TEDtalk

BEing Seen and BEing Heard as a Thought Leader

What's Necessary for Individuals and Businesses to Transition from the Industrial Age to the Social Age.

Mitchell Levy, Eran Levy, Teresa de Grosbois, Robert Clancy, and Swami Sadashiva Tirtha

THiNKaha®

An Actionable Business Journal

E-mail: info@thinkaha.com
20660 Stevens Creek Blvd., Suite 210
Cupertino, CA 95014

Published by THiNKaha®
20660 Stevens Creek Blvd., Suite 210, Cupertino, CA 95014
http://thinkaha.com
E-mail: info@thinkaha.com

First Printing: March 2018
Hardcover ISBN: 978-1-61699-246-0 1-61699-246-8
Paperback ISBN: 978-1-61699-245-3 1-61699-245-X
eBook ISBN: 978-1-61699-244-6 1-61699-244-1
Place of Publication: Silicon Valley, California, USA
Paperback Library of Congress Number: 2018901399

Trademarks

All terms mentioned in this book that are known to be trademarks or service marks have been appropriately capitalized. Neither THiNKaha, nor any of its imprints, can attest to the accuracy of this information. Use of a term in this book should not be regarded as affecting the validity of any trademark or service mark.

Warning and Disclaimer

Every effort has been made to make this book as complete and as accurate as possible. The information provided is on an "as is" basis. The author(s), publisher, and their agents assume no responsibility for errors or omissions. Nor do they assume liability or responsibility to any person or entity with respect to any loss or damages arising from the use of information contained herein.

Acknowledgements

First, I want to acknowledge my wife, Alex, for being such a great partner in life. If I have a wacky idea of what to do with the business, she'll support me. She knows when to push back and helps me hit the humble button. She has given me insight into human nature that has allowed me to serve my customer base better. I wouldn't be the person I am today without her.

Second, I want to acknowledge my son, Duncan (currently nineteen), who has given me insight on where the younger generation is going and how it will affect the business world.

Third, I want to acknowledge my clients and partners who have allowed me to grow, learn, experiment, fail, and through these efforts, come up with a platform that will facilitate the transition from the industrial to the social age.

Dedication

This book is dedicated to Jenilee Maniti, who has helped me deliver many of the wacky ideas I come up with and ensures that our clients have a stellar experience.

How to Read a THiNKaha® Book
A Note from the Publisher

The THiNKaha series is the CliffsNotes of the 21st century. The value of these books is that they are contextual in nature. Although the actual words won't change, their meaning will change every time you read one as your context will change. Experience your own "AHA!" moments ("AHAmessages™") with a THiNKaha book; AHAmessages are looked at as "actionable" moments—think of a specific project you're working on, an event, a sales deal, a personal issue, etc. and see how the AHAmessages in this book can inspire your own AHAmessages, something that you can specifically act on. Here's how to read one of these books and have it work for you:

1. Read a THiNKaha book (these slim and handy books should only take about 15–20 minutes of your time!) and write down one to three actionable items you thought of while reading it. Each journal-style THiNKaha book is equipped with space for you to write down your notes and thoughts underneath each AHAmessage.

2. Mark your calendar to re-read this book again in 30 days.

3. Repeat step #1 and write down one to three more AHAmessages that grab you this time. I guarantee that they will be different than the first time. BTW: this is also a great time to reflect on the actions taken from the last set of AHAmessages you wrote down.

After reading a THiNKaha book, writing down your AHAmessages, re-reading it, and writing down more AHAmessages, you'll begin to see how these books contextually apply to you. THiNKaha books advocate for continuous, lifelong learning. They will help you transform your ahas into actionable items with tangible results until you no longer have to say "AHA!" to these moments—they'll become part of your daily practice as you continue to grow and learn.

As The AHA Guy at THiNKaha, I definitely practice what I preach. I read 2-3 AHAbooks a month in addition to those that we publish and take away two to three different action items from each of them every time. Please e-mail me your AHAs today!

Mitchell Levy
publisher@thinkaha.com

THiNKaha®

Contents

Introduction

I wonder what it was like for individuals when the horse and buggy made way for the automobile and when people moved in mass from the farms to the cities. How many people recognized the changing nature of society and were able to take advantage of it? How many people didn't?

We're in the largest transition the world has ever gone through, as we transition from the industrial age to the social age. I'm wondering how many people see it and are preparing for it.

What's In: customer service, a "Yelp-Score" of the seller customized to those similar to the buyer, individualized sales and marketing, thought leadership, social media, fewer employees, more contractors, cross-cultural work groups, and a computer app for everything.

What's Out: mass marketing and not caring about your customers or the rules they live by.

As a Silicon Valley veteran, I've seen many shifts in technology and the resulting havoc and lost work of tens of thousands of people.

On top of the changing skills needed, we're seeing competitors from around the world. Everyone who wants a microphone can have one, and there's lots of content to sift through.

Should you stand out? YES! If you're not seen in the social age, you will be passed over for someone who is. #AreYouSeen

How do you stand out? How can you be seen and heard as a thought leader? Feel free to watch my TED talk (http://aha.pub/TEDtalk) before reading this book—and then watch it again afterward. If you read the book before watching the TEDtalk, reread the book after watching it, as the context of what you read will have changed. Either way, jot down your AHA moments as you process this wisdom. Then do something about it!

We all need to change what we do and how we do it. I want you to be successful!

If you have an AHA that you don't know what to do about, please reach out. One way to clarify your thought process is to write an AHAbook. The three-step authoring process will help you clarify your thoughts and resulting actions (http://AHAthat.com/Author). If you want help, let us write it for you and have me conduct the interview. Please ask for Mitchell Levy when submitting your order at http://aha.pub/BeSeenPackages.

Good luck creating an environment for yourself where work equals play and you do what you want, when and where you want to do it!

Share the AHA messages from this book socially by going to
http://aha.pub/ThoughtLeadership.

Section I

What Is a Thought Leader and Why Should You Be One?

Thought leaders are recognized experts in their field. They bring ideas to the table that can improve the way things are done. They bring change—good change—and it's their duty to help others reach their potential. Thought leaders lead with their hearts and succeed together with their team. Why should you be one? It's simple: when everyone has a microphone, you need to stand out to survive.

1

Read "BEing Seen and BEing Heard
as a Thought Leader" & share relevant
AHAmessages.
http://aha.pub/ThoughtLeadership
@HappyAbout

_____

_____

_____

2

Watch Mitchell Levy's TED talk on
"BEing Seen and BEing Heard as a Thought
Leader." http://aha.pub/TEDtalk
@HappyAbout

_____

_____

_____

3

The #ThoughtLeaders of the world are the ones always looking for a new and better way of doing things. @TeresaDee

_____

_____

_____

4

Good #ThoughtLeaders are at the top of the mountain; great thought leaders are at the bottom, helping others climb up. @GuideToSoul

_____

_____

_____

5

Good #ThoughtLeaders carry others on their shoulders. If they are at the top, they lend a hand to pull others up. @GuideToSoul

_____

_____

_____

6

Being a #ThoughtLeader is about how you can help people be of greater service to others. @TeresaDee

_____

_____

_____

7

Being a #ThoughtLeader means representing yourself appropriately so people can see who you are and what you're about. @HappyAbout

_____

_____

_____

8

Thought Leadership is having and sharing the right content with the right audience. http://aha.pub/tldef @HappyAbout

_____

_____

_____

9

Great #ThoughtLeaders always guide
people to where they need to go.
http://aha.pub/ThoughtLeadership
@GuideToSoul

_____

_____

_____

10

All the greatest #ThoughtLeaders have
taken people to a place worth going, and
that has to come from the heart.
@GuideToSoul

_____

_____

_____

11

#ThoughtLeadership can come out of group think, as it's not always driven by a single individual. @TeresaDee

_____

_____

_____

12

To be a #ThoughtLeader, you need to be what most people aren't: open to challenges and excited about change. @HappyAbout

_____

_____

_____

13

80 percent of the content one should share as a #ThoughtLeader should be somebody else's. http://aha.pub/ThoughtLeadership @HappyAbout

_____

_____

_____

14

Being comfortable with discomfort and the unknown is good. Are you? @HappyAbout

_____

_____

_____

15

#ThoughtLeadership is not smooth sailing for an org to adopt, as it goes against the natural instinct of sales.
http://aha.pub/EranLevy

_____

_____

_____

16

Good #ThoughtLeadership is about the quality & depth of knowledge you share. Don't limit yourself to one area.
http://aha.pub/EranLevy

_____

_____

_____

17

#ThoughtLeaders are recognized as authorities in an area & are included early in the conversation with clients.
http://aha.pub/EranLevy

_____

_____

_____

18

Good #ThoughtLeadership drives change by interacting with clients and helping change their mindset.
http://aha.pub/EranLevy

_____

_____

_____

19

Resarch is key. Good #ThoughtLeadership is always based on fresh insights. Are you doing enough? http://aha.pub/EranLevy

_____

_____

_____

20

#ThoughtLeadership is about changing the conversation from "I, we, us, our" to "you and your." http://aha.pub/ThoughtLeadership @HappyAbout

_____

_____

_____

Share the AHA messages from this book socially by going to
http://aha.pub/ThoughtLeadership.

Section II

What Should Orgs Do? Empower the Team and Focus on Being a Thought Partner

Thought leadership at the organizational level takes another flavor. Orgs should focus on conducting fundamental research and producing #ThoughtLeadership that their clients can't get elsewhere. The goal is to be recognized as a #ThoughtPartner and be asked to be part of their clients' future planning activities. Additionally, orgs need to make sure that their people are in sync with each other to work productively and smartly.

21

#ThoughtLeadership in a corporate world builds a long-term asset. Are you building? http://aha.pub/EranLevy

_____

_____

_____

22

#ThoughtPartnership means being perceived as a partner in your client's initial thinking process. http://aha.pub/EranLevy

_____

_____

_____

23

The goal of #ThoughtPartnership is to support your client's thought processes. http://aha.pub/EranLevy

_____

_____

_____

24

Don't you want your org to be involved
in the thinking process with your clients?
#ThoughtPartnership
http://aha.pub/EranLevy

_____

_____

_____

25

Sales reps need to be taught the
conversation they should have in order to
be perceived as their customers' thought
partner. http://aha.pub/EranLevy

_____

_____

_____

26

As a #ThoughtPartner, you should help other orgs see where the future might be going, to help them from disappearing. @HappyAbout

_____

_____

_____

27

When clients show you their problems and you share your knowledge, you're perceived as a #ThoughtPartner.
http://aha.pub/EranLevy

28

To position your org as a #ThoughtPartner, bring your key #ThoughtLeaders out front and share their efforts.
http://aha.pub/EranLevy

29

Expand your #ThoughtLeadership scope. Don't limit yourself or it will be perceived as self-serving. http://aha.pub/EranLevy

_____

_____

_____

30

Your team has their own ideas. Ask them. Integrate those ideas and march forward together. #ThoughtPartnership http://aha.pub/EranLevy

_____

_____

_____

31

If you drive a positive #ThoughtPartnership
change across the entire org, you will be
able to close big deals.
http://aha.pub/EranLevy

_____

_____

_____

32

If you are perceived as someone who offers essential insights, you can help execs make better decisions. http://aha.pub/EranLevy

_____

_____

_____

33

The duty of a #ThoughtPartner is to give your clients valuable insights to make better decisions. http://aha.pub/EranLevy

_____

_____

_____

34

If #ThoughtPartnership is done right, your clients consult with you prior to making decisions. http://aha.pub/EranLevy

_____

_____

_____

35

When you deploy something new, you want to minimize risk. People look for partners who know how. Do you? http://aha.pub/EranLevy

_____

_____

_____

36

Business is not about business; it's about people. http://aha.pub/ThoughtLeadership @GuideToSoul

_____

_____

_____

37

Helping others should apply in both our personal and business lives. Are you helping others? http://aha.pub/TEDtalk @HappyAbout

_____

_____

_____

38

If you make your community connection a part of the mantra of your company, you'll be able to help people more. @GuideToSoul

_____

_____

_____

39

You got to bring humor into it.
If you don't have some laughter in the office,
you've lost everything.
http://aha.pub/ThoughtLeadership
@GuideToSoul

_____

_____

_____

40

The reason people work together is because they want to work toward something good. Give them that reason! @GuideToSoul

_____

_____

_____

41

Make your #ThoughtLeadership go broad because it helps cement yourself as a #ThoughtPartner. http://aha.pub/EranLevy

_____

_____

_____

42

Influence is amplified through your relationships with other influential people. Who are you connected to? @TeresaDee

_____

_____

_____

43

Everyone has good attributes. Compliment others on theirs. #Compensation http://aha.pub/ThoughtLeadership @HappyAbout

---

44

If someone you're working with should use another org, recommend that -- it's the long-term relationship that counts. @HappyAbout

---

45

The world will shift; there are orgs that won't stay on top, and disappear. Are you on top of things? http://aha.pub/EranLevy

_____

_____

_____

46

Who are you as a company? You're the sum of your parts. Now the question is, "How do you make the whole better?" @HappyAbout

_____

_____

_____

Share the AHA messages from this book socially by going to
http://aha.pub/ThoughtLeadership.

Section III

We Learn, We Grow

Learning doesn't stop when you finish school; it's a continuous exercise that has no end as long as you're alive. Why do we need to continue learning? Because it helps us be better each day. Continuous learning is important for thought leaders, as they must have the knowledge to be recognized and to influence those in their circles to make an impact.

47

Life is about continuous improvement.
Are you constantly improving yourself?
@HappyAbout

_____

_____

_____

48

Every person has their own genius! What's
yours? http://aha.pub/ThoughtLeadership
@MonkMedium

_____

_____

_____

49

We all have that "hero's journey." Grow into your own maturity, and hit that goal you've been aspiring to. @MonkMedium

_____

_____

_____

50

Take what you've learned,
and push yourself to take bigger risks
to help more people in a bigger way.
http://aha.pub/ThoughtLeadership
@MonkMedium

_____

_____

_____

51

When you're knocked down and there's no one there but you, just pick yourself up -- nobody else will. @MonkMedium

_____

_____

_____

52

You don't win at the degree of life by thinking that you'll get by on a single skill set or area of personal growth. @TeresaDee

_____

_____

_____

53

You don't necessarily need to be knocked
down to be able to come back up. Be ready.
Look and strive for a better life!
@HappyAbout

_____

_____

_____

54

What are the interesting elements that help you be you? Are you enhancing them daily? @HappyAbout

_____

_____

_____

55

You might fail at everything, but if you try, you at least have a chance at success. http://aha.pub/ThoughtLeadership @GuideToSoul

_____

_____

_____

56

#ThoughtLeadership is where skill meets desire. The world runs on more than good intentions; constantly invest in yourself.
@TeresaDee

_____

_____

_____

57

If you're in the realm of #ThoughtLeadership, you better be investing in the skills that are required. Are you? @TeresaDee

_____

_____

_____

58

To be a leader of leaders, you need to give up the idea that you're the smartest person in the room at any given moment.
@TeresaDee

_____

_____

_____

59

Dedicated lifelong learning is important. When you stop learning and growing, it's the start of a slow march to the grave.
@TeresaDee

_____

_____

_____

60

Amateur practice is until you get it right,
and professional practice is until you can't
get it wrong. How do you practice?
@TeresaDee

_____

_____

_____

61

Whatever scenario you're in, train yourself
to be exquisite in that scenario in order to
be of high service to others. @TeresaDee

_____

_____

_____

62

None of us are ever done; all of us are works in progress. Are you?
http://aha.pub/TEDtalk @TeresaDee

_____

_____

_____

63

Change is uncomfortable, yet discomfort is the doorway to breakthroughs. @TeresaDee

_____

_____

_____

Share the AHA messages from this book socially by going to
http://aha.pub/ThoughtLeadership.

Section IV

We Do Business with Those We Know, Like, and Trust

It's an inevitable fact that people do business and purchase from those they have confidence in: those they know, like, and trust. If you think about it, most people don't do business with someone they're uncomfortable with. As an industry leader, you need to learn how to foster people to know, like, and trust you in order for them to have confidence in you, your company, and your products and services.

64

Be you, and the right person will see you, trust you, and show up to work with you. http://aha.pub/TEDtalk @MonkMedium

_____

_____

_____

65

Be honest and transparent. You don't need to be perfect. Accept your flaws, fix them, and be open to suggestions. @HappyAbout

_____

_____

_____

66

If you keep on pretending to be someone else, no matter how hard you try, it's never going to work. @MonkMedium

_____

_____

_____

67

If you start off a presentation w/ a joke, everybody is on your side. They may not agree w/ your belief, but they like you.
@MonkMedium

_____

_____

_____

68

Want to earn other people's trust? Then show them who you really are as a person.
http://aha.pub/TEDtalk @HappyAbout #Authenticity

_____

_____

_____

69

Become a person of #Integrity. It happens when you say you're going to do something and you actually do what you say. @HappyAbout

_____

_____

_____

70

Be authentic! Present who you are, not who you think other people want to see you as. http://aha.pub/TEDtalk @HappyAbout

_____

_____

_____

71

Trust stems from authenticity, integrity, and
vulnerability. Do you live all three?
http://aha.pub/ThoughtLeadership
@MonkMedium @HappyAbout

_____

_____

_____

72

1 of 3 things you need to demonstrate
in order to earn other people's trust:
#Vulnerability. http://aha.pub/TEDtalk
@HappyAbout @MonkMedium

_____

_____

_____

73

2 of 3 things you need to demonstrate in order to earn other people's trust: #Integrity. http://aha.pub/TEDtalk @HappyAbout @MonkMedium

_____

_____

_____

74

3 of 3 things you need to demonstrate in order to earn other people's trust: #Authenticity. http://aha.pub/TEDtalk @HappyAbout @MonkMedium

_____

_____

_____

75

Are you being you? Are you being authentic and showing integrity and vulnerability? How can people trust you if you don't?
@HappyAbout

_____

_____

_____

76

We don't need to know how we're going to serve others. Have the intention to care & show up. There'll be opportunity to serve. @MonkMedium

_____

_____

_____

77

Make sure all expectations are clear so it's a win-win situation for everyone and worth everyone's time. @TeresaDee

_____

_____

_____

78

Generating trust means that you have to live in a space of integrity, authenticity, and vulnerability. http://aha.pub/TEDtalk @HappyAbout

---

79

People often have false expectations. Stand in integrity, and make sure people are clear with what they can expect from you. @TeresaDee

---

80

A part of integrity is not leaving
things unsaid. Say what needs
to be said in the given moment.
http://aha.pub/ThoughtLeadership
@TeresaDee

_____

_____

_____

81

Breakdowns happen not because things
weren't set correctly, but because things
weren't set at all. @TeresaDee

_____

_____

_____

82

If your heart isn't in what you're saying, you'll fall flat and nobody will listen to you. @TeresaDee

_____

_____

_____

83

People want to do business w/ people they know, like & trust. How do you gain & garner that knowledge, like & trust? @HappyAbout

_____

_____

_____

Share the AHA messages from this book socially by going to
http://aha.pub/ThoughtLeadership.

Section V

Thought Leadership with Passion

Thought Leadership is not easy. It takes more than knowledge and position to be a thought leader. Your leadership needs to come from the heart, and you need to have a sincere passion for helping others succeed. If you lead with love and passion in your heart, the people you're leading will feel your willingness and honesty and want to become better themselves.

84

If you love your job, you'll never work a day in your life. If your job is loving, you'll work in happiness every day. @GuideToSoul

_____

_____

_____

85

The more passionate you are, the quicker
you attract what you're wanting.
http://aha.pub/ThoughtLeadership
@MonkMedium

_____

_____

_____

86

Empathy = going into the pit to hug someone; compassion = pulling someone out of the pit and then embracing them. @GuideToSoul

_____

_____

_____

87

Compassion is understanding a person and what they're going through and letting them know that they matter. @GuideToSoul

_____

_____

_____

88

When love is in your heart, life will mend itself. But if love is in your soul, you can mend the hearts of others. @GuideToSoul

_____

_____

_____

89

LOVE = Leadership, Opportunity, Volunteerism, Enthusiasm. @GuideToSoul

_____

_____

_____

90

Compassion is saying, "I can help you. We're going to do this and work together." @GuideToSoul

_____

_____

_____

91

Love is about being open; we need to take the gloves off and be real from this point forward. @GuideToSoul

_____

_____

_____

92

In today's world, anyone can be a #ThoughtLeader, at any time, of anything you have passion, interest, and time for. @HappyAbout

_____

_____

_____

93

Be who you really want to be. Why wait till tomorrow, when you could start today? http://aha.pub/ThoughtLeadership @HappyAbout

_____

_____

_____

94

When you start looking at what your life
may look like if you lived the way you
wanted, many possibilities open up.
@TeresaDee

_____

_____

_____

95

How we create things is all in the context we want to put them in and the words we want to create around them. @TeresaDee

_____

_____

_____

96

Transform a negative attitude into a positive one. You'll live a happier life.
http://aha.pub/ThoughtLeadership
@HappyAbout

_____

_____

_____

97

To transform a negative attitude into a positive one, you need to recognize and figure it out and believe in yourself. @HappyAbout

_____

_____

_____

98

Will you call this stressful and horrible? Or will you call it exciting and courageous? That's really up to you. @TeresaDee

_____

_____

_____

99

Does your salesforce have knowledge & a desire to solve problems, or do they just want to sell something?
http://aha.pub/EranLevy

_____

_____

_____

100

What context do you want to create for your life? Make it one of purpose and significance.
http://aha.pub/ThoughtLeadership
@TeresaDee

_____

_____

_____

101

Give yourself permission to step into your dreams and take action, because until you take action, you're just dreaming.
@TeresaDee

_____

_____

_____

Share the AHA messages from this book socially by going to
http://aha.pub/ThoughtLeadership.

Section VI

BE Seen and BE Heard

Being seen and being heard as a Thought Leader can be difficult. You must be able to capture people's attention and truly understand that "you're the focal point!" With the help of many social media platforms, your voice can reach millions. As a thought leader, you want to be recognized as an expert in your field, as someone people can turn to and count on, and as someone who people know, like, and trust.

102

Be the right voice for the right person at the right time. Don't underestimate what you bring to the world by being you.
@GuideToSoul

_____

_____

_____

103

Be happy, keep smiling, and stay wonderful by getting your message to the heart of people. http://aha.pub/ThoughtLeadership
@MonkMedium

_____

_____

_____

104

Want your audience to see you
the way you need to be seen?
Then create your own AHAmessages at
https://AHAthat.com/Author!
@HappyAbout

_____

_____

_____

105

These days, "being seen" means we need
to lead from our hearts. This involves
authenticity, vulnerability, and joy.
@MonkMedium

_____

_____

_____

106

Giving yourself a new framework that works is like giving yourself a new set of eyeglasses to view your existing situation. @HappyAbout

_____

_____

_____

107

You don't have to know how you're going to serve people. You just have to have the intention, commitment & heart to help them. @MonkMedium

_____

_____

_____

108

The mechanics of showing up to be seen is with your heart saying, "How can I serve?" @MonkMedium

_____

_____

_____

109

We all need to be able to live in our hearts so the people around us see who we really are. @HappyAbout

_____

_____

_____

110

Each of us has a unique journey in life -- we have a unique voice & perspective. Be yourself & share that with the world. @GuideToSoul

_____

_____

_____

111

Being seen and being heard is knowing
who's on the other side, their expectations,
and making sure you're aligned.
@HappyAbout

_____

_____

_____

112

If what you're saying is important, it's important enough to learn how to say it well. http://aha.pub/ThoughtLeadership @TeresaDee

_____

_____

_____

113

Take the time to learn how to say your speech well and impactfully so people can step in to what you're doing. @TeresaDee

_____

_____

_____

114

You'll know if you've practiced enough times for a speech when your head and heart are both in the messaging.
@TeresaDee

_____

_____

_____

115

What's relevant in #ThoughtLeadership is not only being someone who can answer the question but also being recognized as such. @HappyAbout

_____

_____

_____

116

Not everyone has an opinion that will cause you to want to change. Everyone has an opinion you have to listen to. @HappyAbout

_____

_____

_____

117

How do you have relationships with people so word-of-mouth epidemics can start to spread around your own work? @TeresaDee

_____

_____

_____

118

It takes more than desire to be someone who stands for helping other people change their belief systems and attitudes. @TeresaDee

_____

_____

_____

119

To be successful, you must have community and vision. It has to be more than whatever it is you're doing to make money.
@HappyAbout

_____

_____

_____

120

You must have more than desire to succeed. You need the commitment to learn good skill sets that will help get you there. @TeresaDee

_____

_____

_____

121

Go out there and be as successful
as you can, and then make that
difference with your success.
http://aha.pub/ThoughtLeadership
@GuideToSoul

_____

_____

_____

Share the AHA messages from this book socially by going to
http://aha.pub/ThoughtLeadership.

Section VII

Connecting with People and Making a Difference

How can you make a difference in other people's lives? You first need to be able to connect with them at a core level. Connecting with people and creating a meaningful relationship with them is a great way to earn their trust. Once they trust you, you have a better opportunity to influence their work and personal life. Thought leaders make a difference.

122

Want to help and make a difference?
Start by touching people's hearts.
http://aha.pub/ThoughtLeadership
@MonkMedium

_____

_____

_____

123

If you shine your light, your people will follow. --Susan Kirby via @HappyAbout

_____

_____

_____

124

Want to change the world?
Then start by helping people feel better.
http://aha.pub/ThoughtLeadership
@MonkMedium

_____

_____

_____

125

Keep moving forward. Don't avoid getting
knocked down. Release the genius in you!
@MonkMedium

_____

_____

_____

126

What's your favorite movie? Think about the story behind it, why you connect to it, then write it down. @MonkMedium

_____

_____

_____

127

Be part of the world to become part of everything. http://aha.pub/ThoughtLeadership @GuideToSoul

_____

_____

_____

128

Endorse the businesses in your community and #GetInvolved. When you do that, you can make a difference. @GuideToSoul

_____

_____

_____

129

Embrace the community you're living in. That's where your roots are and where you get your nourishment. @GuideToSoul

_____

_____

_____

130

Where you plant yourself is where you grow.
#EmbraceYourCommunity @GuideToSoul

_____

_____

_____

131

We have one world and one heart -- that's
why we need to be in touch with everything.
@GuideToSoul

_____

_____

_____

132

Inspire people to try something different and do something new.
http://aha.pub/ThoughtLeadership
@TeresaDee

_____

_____

_____

133

Social media is two words: "Social" and "Media." When deploying social media, 80% of what you focus on should be social.
@HappyAbout

_____

_____

_____

134

If somebody likes or shares your content on social, find a way to say http://aha.pub/ThankYou! @HappyAbout

_____

_____

_____

135

If you know who you are, then you'll recognize things others have done well & give them attribution. Do you? @TeresaDee

_____

_____

_____

136

Relationships are born in cycles of reciprocity. Try having deep relationships that support one another. http://aha.pub/ThoughtLeadership @TeresaDee

_____

_____

_____

137

When you're committed to causing change in the world, you will practice hard, even if it means practicing 400 or 500 times.
@TeresaDee

_____

_____

_____

138

Life always brings you choices. You get to choose a framework that allows you to get to the place you really want to be. @HappyAbout

_____

_____

_____

139

There are great companies out there making a difference in the world. Are you part of one? @GuideToSoul

_____

_____

_____

140

As we're now moving to the social age, we
need to realize that we need to #Collaborate
with each other in order to grow.
http://aha.pub/TEDtalk
@HappyAbout

_____

_____

_____

About the Authors

MITCHELL LEVY

Mitchell Levy, @HappyAbout, is The AHA Guy & CEO at AHAthat who empowers thought leaders to share their genius. He is an accomplished Entrepreneur who has created twenty businesses in Silicon Valley including four publishing companies that have published over 800 books. Mitchell is a TEDx speaker and international bestselling author with fifty-nine business books. He's provided strategic consulting to over one hundred companies, has advised over five hundred CEOs on critical business issues, and has been chairman of the board of a NASDAQ-listed company. In addition to these accomplishments, he's been happily married for twenty-eight years and regularly spends four weeks annually in a European country with his family and friends.

ERAN LEVY

••••••••••••••••••••••••••••••••

Eran Levy
(**http://aha.pub/EranLevy**)
is the Executive Director of
Connected Futures
(**https://connectedfutures.cisco.
com/bio/eran-levy/**) and the
head of Cisco's C-Suite Thought
Leadership group. He directs
original research and reporting
aimed at helping executives
create business value through
technology. His background
includes positions in engineering,
product management, and
business development at leading
technology companies.

TERESA DE GROSBOIS

••••••••••••••••••••••••••••••••

Teresa de Grosbois
@TeresaDee is the Chair of the
Evolutionary Business Council
(**https://ebcouncil.com/**) and
an international speaker sought
by entrepreneurs and large
corporations wanting to better
understand how local gossip
can suddenly turn into epidemic
word of mouth. Specializing
in the topics of influence and
success, she has a proven track
record in understanding word-of-
mouth epidemics, having taken
three books to bestseller status in
only eight months. Teresa teaches
business and marketing courses
around the globe, including
teaching courses to startup
entrepreneurs in developing
countries.

ROBERT CLANCY

· · · · · · · · · · · · · · · · · · ·

Robert Clancy
@GuideToSoul is the bestselling author of the book, *Soul Cyphers*, and a co-founder and managing partner of Spiral Design (**https://spiraldesign.com/**), a graphic design and web development firm that specializes in taking corporate brands, marketing campaigns, and website design from ordinary to extraordinary. Robert supports ongoing volunteerism in business and his everyday life. His dedication to others at both the regional and national levels inspires his team and encourages other professional leaders to step up and give back.

SWAMI SADASHIVA TIRTHA

· · · · · · · · · · · · · · · · · · ·

Swami Sadashiva Tirtha
@MonkMedium,
aka The Orange Cowboy
(**http://orangecowboy.com**), is a born shaman and healer whose life calling is to share light, love, and joy with people around the world. He has presented to the White House Commission on alternative medicine and has been teaching wellness and consciousness for over four decades. Sadashiva has also written several books, including an Amazon number-one bestseller, *The Ayurveda Encyclopedia*.

AHAthat™

AHAthat makes it easy to share, author, and promote content. There are over 40,000 quotes (AHAmessages™) by thought leaders from around the world that you can share in seconds for free.

For those who want to author their own book, we have time-tested proven processes that allow you to write your AHAbook™ of 140 digestible, bite-sized morsels in eight hours or less. Once your content is on AHAthat, you have a customized link that you can use to have your fans/advocates share your content and help grow your network.

⮑ Start sharing: **https://AHAthat.com**

⮑ Start authoring: **https://AHAthat.com/Author**

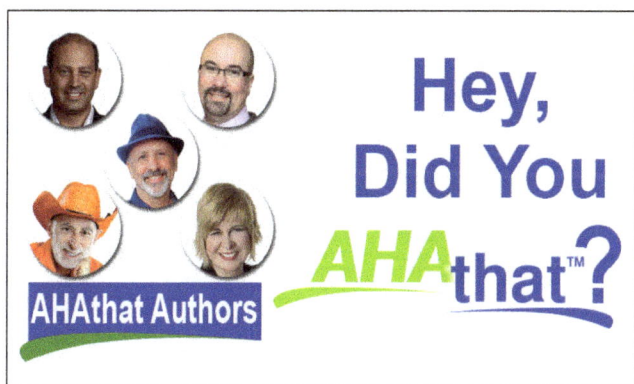

Please go directly to this book in AHAthat and share each AHAmessage socially at
http://aha.pub/ThoughtLeadership.